FUN FAC
Scienc

Terry O'Brien is an academician by ᴗn and a passionate quiz enthusiast by avocation. His leitmotif is the igniting of the quizzing instinct and an aptitude to develop the 3Rs of learning: Read. Record. Recall. He is a trainer's trainer and a motivational speaker who has written several books. His flair for writing and speaking comes naturally to him.

By the same author

Little Red Book Series

Little Red Book of Slang-Chat Room Slang	Little Red Book of Modern Writing Skills
Little Red Book of English Vocabulary Today	Little Red Book of Verbal Phrases
Little Red Book of Grammar Made Easy	Little Red Book of Synonyms
Little Red Book of English Proverbs	Little Red Book of Antonyms
Little Red Book of Prepositions	Little Red Book of Common Errors
Little Red Book of Idioms and Phrases	Little Red Book of Letter Writing
Little Red Book of Euphemisms	Little Red Book of Perfect Written English
Little Red Book of Effective Speaking Skills	Little Red Book of Essay Writing
	Little Red Book of Word Fact
	Little Red Book of Spelling
	Little Red Book of Language Checklist

Fun Series

Fun Facts Animals	Fun with Riddles
Fun Facts India	Fun with Math
Fun Facts Nature	Fun with Puzzles
	Fun with Numbers

Classic Tales for Children

Adventure Stories for Children	Bravery Stories for Children
Mystery Stories for Children	Detective Stories for Children
School Stories for Children	Funny Stories for Children
Animal Stories for Children	Scary Stories for Children

A2Z Book Series

A2Z Quiz Book	A2Z Book of Word Origins

Others

The Book of Fun Facts	The Book of Motivation
The Book of More Fun Facts	Read Write Right: Common Errors in English
The Book of Firsts and Lasts	The Students' Companion
The Book of Virtues	
World Facts Finder	

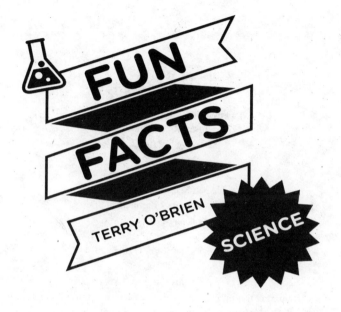

FUN
FACTS

TERRY O'BRIEN

SCIENCE

RUPA

Published by
Rupa Publications India Pvt. Ltd 2013
7/16, Ansari Road, Daryaganj
New Delhi 110002

Sales centres:
Allahabad Bengaluru Chennai
Hyderabad Jaipur Kathmandu
Kolkata Mumbai

Edition copyright © Terry O'Brien 2013

ISBN: 978-81-291-2922-2

Second impression 2015

10 9 8 7 6 5 4 3 2

The moral right of the author has been asserted.

Printed at Rakmo Press Pvt. Ltd, New Delhi

Introduction

Learning can be fun! Children can learn to make sense of the world around them. Through fun facts, children can develop social and cognitive skills and gain the self-confidence required to engage in new experiences and environments:

- Fun Facts must be pleasurable and enjoyable.
- Fun Facts must have no extrinsic goals; there is no prescribed learning that must occur.
- Fun Facts is spontaneous and voluntary.
- Fun Facts involves active engagement on the part of the reader.
- Fun Facts involve an element of make-believe.

'Edutainment' is a new approach for all to enjoy information that is around us but is often missed by most. This involves both play and work. There are differences between play and work. Play is mostly a self-chosen activity by the child, rather than prescribed by a parent or teacher; it is a process, rather than a predicted outcome or product. Work, on the other hand, has a definite intent and a prescribed outcome.

The Fun Facts series is compiled on a strong internally based motivation for playing. If parents and educators try to label experiences as play, but in reality have specific requirements for the activity, then it becomes work not play. Play is not wasted time, but rather time spent building new knowledge from previous experience.

There is a strong link between play and learning for young children, especially in the areas of problem solving, language skills, literacy, social, physical, and emotional skills. Young children actively explore their environment and the world around them through learning-based play. Play is a vital part of a child's optimal social, cognitive, physical and emotional development. Indeed Fun Facts provides a strong foundation for creativity, problem-solving and basic quest for knowledge. Through Fun Facts, children learn a set of skills.

There is indeed a positive co-relation between play and children's learning. Thus, we have edutainment! The true value of edutainment is not that it can teach children facts, but that it can help them acquire important procedural knowledge, which is beneficial in acquiring declarative knowledge.

Today is a world of information boom. So we are ready for Infotainment, combining information with entertainment.

Happy reading!

FUN FACTS: SCIENCE

MIXED BAG

There are 62,000 miles of blood vessels in the human body – laid end to end they would circle the earth 2.5 times.

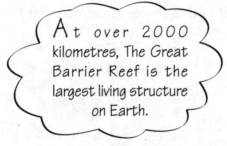

At over 2000 kilometres, The Great Barrier Reef is the largest living structure on Earth.

The risk of being struck by a falling meteorite for a human is one occurrence every 9,300 years.

A thimbleful of a neutron star would weigh over 100 million tons.

A typical hurricane produces the energy equivalent of 8,000 one megaton bombs.

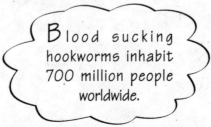

Blood sucking hookworms inhabit 700 million people worldwide.

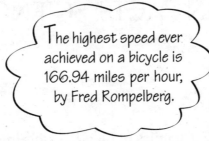

The highest speed ever achieved on a bicycle is 166.94 miles per hour, by Fred Rompelberg.

We can produce laser light a million times brighter than sunshine.

65 per cent of those with autism are left-handed.

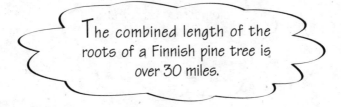

The combined length of the roots of a Finnish pine tree is over 30 miles.

The oceans contain enough salt to cover all the continents to a depth of nearly 500 feet.

The interstellar gas cloud Sagittarius B contains a billion, billion, billion litres of alcohol. Frater is planning to move there in the near future.

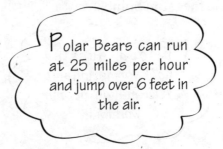

Polar Bears can run at 25 miles per hour and jump over 6 feet in the air.

60-65 million years ago, dolphins and humans shared a common ancestor.

Polar Bears are nearly undetectable by infrared cameras, due to their transparent fur.

The average person accidentally eats 430 bugs each year of his life.

A single rye plant can spread up to 400 miles of roots underground.

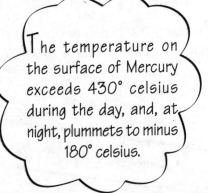

The temperature on the surface of Mercury exceeds 430° celsius during the day, and, at night, plummets to minus 180° celsius.

The evaporation from a large oak or beech tree is from 10 to 25 gallons in twenty four hours.

Butterflies taste with their hind feet, and their taste sensation works on touch. This allows them to determine whether a leaf is edible.

MORE SCIENCE

The speed of light is generally rounded down to 186,000 miles per second. In exact terms it is 299,792,458 m/s (metres per second)—that is equal to 186,287.49 miles per second.

> It takes eight minutes seventeen seconds for light to travel from the Sun's surface to the Earth.

Ten per cent of all human beings ever born are alive at this very moment.

The Earth spins at 1,000 miles per hour but it travels through space at an incredible 67,000 miles per hour.

> Every year, over one million earthquakes shake the Earth.

The largest ever hailstone weighed over 1 kilogram and fell in Bangladesh in 1986.

Every second, around 100 lightning bolts strike the Earth.

Every year, lightning kills 1,000 people.

In October 1999, an Iceberg the size of London broke free from the Antarctic ice shelf.

If you could drive your car straight up, you would arrive in space in just over an hour.

Human tapeworms can grow up to 22.9 metres.

The Earth is 4.56 billion years old…the same age as the Moon and the Sun.

Dinosaurs became extinct before the Rockies or the Alps were formed.

Female black widow spiders eat their males after mating.

When a flea jumps, the rate of acceleration is twenty times that of a space shuttle during launch.

If our sun were just an inch in diameter, the nearest star would be 445 miles away.

Astronauts cannot belch—there is no gravity to separate liquid from gas in their stomachs.

The air at the summit of Mount Everest, 29,029 feet is only a third as thick as the air at sea level.

> One million, million, million, million, millionth of a second after the Big Bang, the Universe was the size of a pea.

DNA was first discovered in 1869 by Swiss Friedrich Mieschler.

The molecular structure of DNA was first determined by Watson and Crick in 1953.

The first synthetic human chromosome was constructed by US scientists in 1997.

The thermometer was invented in 1607 by Galileo.

Englishman Roger Bacon invented the magnifying glass in 1250.

> Alfred Nobel invented dynamite in 1866.

Wilhelm Rontgen won the first Nobel Prize for physics for discovering X-rays in 1895.

Christiaan Barnard performed the first heart transplant in 1967 – the patient lived for eighteen days.

An electric eel can produce a shock of up to 650 volts.

Wireless communications took a giant leap forward in 1962 with the launch of Telstar, the first satellite capable of relaying telephone and satellite TV signals.

Giraffes often sleep for only twenty minutes in any twenty four hours. They may sleep up to two hours (in spurts – not all at once), but this is rare. They never lie down.

Without its lining of mucus your stomach would digest itself.

Humans have forty six chromosomes, peas have fourteen and crayfish have 200.

There are 60,000 miles of blood vessels in the human body.

An individual blood cell takes about sixty seconds to make a complete circuit of the body.

On the day that Alexander Graham Bell was buried, the entire US telephone system was shut down for one minute in tribute.

The low frequency call of the humpback whale is the loudest noise made by a living creature.

The call of the humpback whale is louder than Concorde and can be heard from 500 miles away.

A quarter of the world's plants were threatened with extinction by the year 2010.

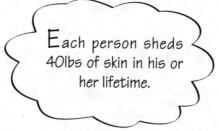

Each person sheds 40lbs of skin in his or her lifetime.

At 15 inches, the eyes of giant squids are the largest on the planet.

The largest galaxies contain a million, million stars.

The Universe contains over 100 billion galaxies.

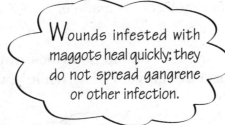

Wounds infested with maggots heal quickly; they do not spread gangrene or other infection.

More germs are transferred while shaking hands than kissing.

The fastest speed at which a falling raindrop can hit you is 18 miles per hour.

A healthy person has 6,000 million, million, million haemoglobin molecules.

Inbreeding causes three out of every ten Dalmation dogs to suffer from hearing disability.

The world's smallest winged insect, the Tanzanian parasitic wasp, is smaller than the eye of a housefly.

It would take over an hour for a heavy object to sink 6.7 miles down to the deepest part of the ocean.

There are more living organisms on the skin of each human than there are humans on the surface of the earth.

Each rubber molecule is made of 65,000 individual atoms.

Around a million, billion neutrinos from the Sun will pass through your body while you read this sentence.

The saturn V rocket which carried man to the Moon, develops power equivalent to fifty 747 jumbo jets.

Koalas sleep an average of twenty two hours a day, two hours more than the sloth.

Light would take .13 seconds to travel around the Earth.

Males produce one thousand sperm cells each second —86 million each day.

Neutron stars are so dense that a teaspoonful would weigh more than all the people on Earth.

One in every 2000 babies is born with a tooth.

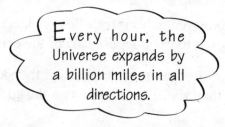

Every hour, the Universe expands by a billion miles in all directions.

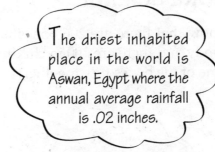

The driest inhabited place in the world is Aswan, Egypt where the annual average rainfall is .02 inches.

The mortality rate if bitten by a Black Mamba snake is over 95 per cent.

90 per cent of those who die from hurricanes die from drowning.

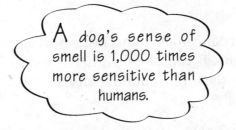

A dog's sense of smell is 1,000 times more sensitive than humans.

To escape the Earth's gravity, a rocket needs to travel at 7 miles a second.

If every star in the Milky Way was a grain of salt, they would fill an Olympic-sized swimming pool.

Microbial life can survive on the cooling rods of a nuclear reactor.

SOME MORE SCIENCE

Did you know that there are 206 bones in the adult human body and there are 300 in children (as they grow some of the bones fuse together).

Flea's can jump 130 times higher than their own height. In human terms' this is equal to a 6 feet person jumping 780 feet in the air.

The most dangerous animal in the world is the common housefly. Because of their habits of visiting animal waste, they transmit more diseases than any other animal.

Snakes are true carnivores because they eat nothing but other animals. They do not eat any type of plant material.

The world's largest amphibian is the giant salamander. It can grow up to 5 feet in length.

100 years ago: The first virus was found in both plants and animals.

Ninety years ago: The Grand Canyon became a national monument and cellophane was invented.

Eighty years ago: The food mixer and the domestic refrigerator were invented.

Seventy years ago: The teletype and PVC (polyvinyl-chloride) were invented.

Sixty years ago: Otto Hahn discovered nuclear fission by splitting uranium; Teflon was invented.

Fifty years ago: Velcro was invented.

Forty years ago: An all-female population of lizards was discovered in Armenia.

Thirty years ago: The computer mouse was invented.

Twenty years ago: The first test-tube baby was born in England; Pluto's moon Charon was discovered.

Ten years ago: The first patent for a genetically-engineered mouse was issued to Harvard Medical School.

> Five years ago: The first human embryo was successfully cloned.

The smallest bone in the human body is the stapes or stirrup bone located in the middle ear. It is approximately .11 inches (.28 centimetres) long.

The longest cells in the human body are the motor neurons. They can be up to 4.5 feet (1.37 metres) long and run from the lower spinal cord to the big toe.

There are no poisonous snakes in Maine.

The blue whale can produce sounds up to 188 decibels. This is the loudest sound produced by a living animal and has been detected from as far away as 530 miles.

The largest man-made lake in the U.S. is Lake Mead, created by Hoover Dam.

> The poison arrow frogs of South and Central America are the most poisonous animals in the world.

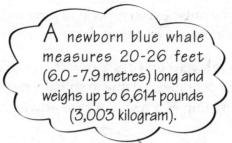

A newborn blue whale measures 20-26 feet (6.0 - 7.9 metres) long and weighs up to 6,614 pounds (3,003 kilogram).

The first coast-to-coast telephone line was established in 1914.

The Virginia opossum has a gestation period of only twelve to thirteen days.

The Stegosaurus dinosaur measured up to 30 feet (9.1 metres) but had a brain the size of a walnut.

The largest meteorite crater in the world is in Winslow, Arizona. It is 4,150 feet across and 150 feet deep.

The human eye blinks an average of 4,200,000 times a year.

Skylab, the first American space station, fell to the earth in thousands of pieces in 1979. Thankfully, most of it over the ocean.

It takes approximately twelve hours for food to digest fully.

Human jaw muscles can generate a force of 200 pounds (90.8 kilograms) on the molars.

The Skylab astronauts grew 1.5 – 2.25 inches (3.8 - 5.7 centimetres) due to spinal lengthening and straightening as a result of zero gravity.

An inch (2.5 centimetres) of rain water is equivalent to 15 inches (38.1 centimetres) of dry, powdery snow.

Tremendous erosion at the base of the Niagara Falls (USA) undermines the shale cliffs and as a result, the falls have receded approximately 7 miles over the last 10,000 years.

40 to 50 per cent of body heat can be lost through the head (no hat) as a result of its extensive circulatory network.

A large swarm of desert locusts (Schistocerca gregaria) can consume 20,000 tons (18,160,000 kilograms) of vegetation a day.

The largest telescope in the world is currently being constructed in Northern Chile. The telescope will utilise four 26 feet 8 inch (8.13 metres) mirrors which will gather as much light as a single 52 feet 6 inch (16 metres) mirror.

The Hubble Space Telescope weighs 12 tons (10,896 kilograms), is 43 feet (13.1 metres) long, and costed $2.1 billion to originally build.

The longest living cells in the body are brain cells which can live an entire lifetime.

The largest flying animal was the Pterosaur which lived 70 million years ago. This reptile had a wing span of 36-39 feet (11-11.9 metres) and weighed 190-250 pounds (86-113.5 kilograms).

The Atlantic Giant Squid's eye can be as large as 15.75 inches (40 centimetres) wide.

Armadillos, opossums, and sloth spend about 80 per cent of their lives sleeping.

The starfish species, Porcellanaster ivanovi, has been found to live in waters as deep as 24,881 feet (7,584 metres).

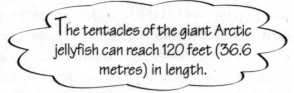

The tentacles of the giant Arctic jellyfish can reach 120 feet (36.6 metres) in length.

The greatest tide change on earth occurs in the Bay of Fundy. The difference between low tide and high tide can be as great as 54 feet 6 inches (16.6 metres).

The highest temperature produced in a laboratory was 920,000,000 °F (511,000,000 °C) at the Tokamak Fusion Test Reactor in Princeton, NJ, USA.

The most powerful laser in the world, the Nova laser at Lawrence Livermore National Laboratory, CA, USA, generates a pulse of energy equal to 100,000,000,000,000 watts of power for .000000001 second to a target the size of a grain of sand.

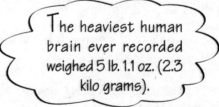

The heaviest human brain ever recorded weighed 5 lb. 1.1 oz. (2.3 kilo grams).

The fastest computer in the world is the CRAY Y-MP C90 supercomputer. It has two gigabytes of central memory and sixteen parallel central processor units.

The deepest part of the ocean is 35,813 feet (10,916 metres) deep and occurs in the Mariana Trench in the Pacific Ocean. At that depth the pressure is 18,000 pounds (9172 kilograms) per square inch.

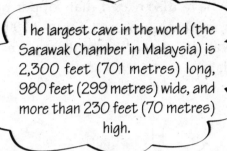

The he largest cave in the world (the Sarawak Chamber in Malaysia) is 2,300 feet (701 metres) long, 980 feet (299 metres) wide, and more than 230 feet (70 metres) high.

The hottest planet in the solar system is Venus, with an estimated surface temperature of 864 °F (462 °C).

The ears of a cricket are located on the front legs, just below the knee.

The first electronic digital computer (called ENIAC - the Electronic Numerical Integrator and Calculator) was developed in 1946 and contained over 18,000 vacuum tubes.

The leg muscles of a locust are about 1000 times more powerful than an equal weight of human muscle.

The cosmos contain approximately 50,000,000,000 galaxies.

Sound travels about four times faster in water than in air.

There are between 100,000,000,000 and 1,000,000,000,000 stars in a normal galaxy.

Scientists have discovered that copper pollution of the atmosphere occurred about 2,500 years ago. This was discovered by analysing ice cores from Greenland.

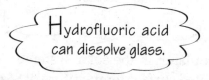

Hydrofluoric acid can dissolve glass.

A large sunspot can last for about a week.

If you could throw a snowball fast enough, it would totally vaporize when it hits a brick wall.

Boron Nitride (BN) is the second hardest substance known to man.

The female Tarantula Hawk wasp paralyses a large spider with her sting. She then lays her eggs on the motionless body so that her developing young have a fresh supply of spider meat to feed on.

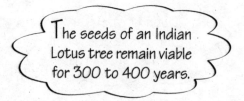

The seeds of an Indian Lotus tree remain viable for 300 to 400 years.

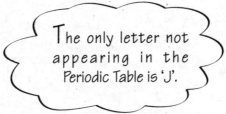

The only letter not appearing in the Periodic Table is 'J'.

Velcro was invented by a Swiss who was inspired by the way burrs attached to clothing.

Hershey's Kisses are called that because the machine that makes them looks like it's kissing the conveyor belt.

October 10 is National Metric Day.

If you stretch a standard Slinky out flat, it measures 87 feet.

The microwave was invented after a researcher walked by a radar tube and a chocolate bar melted in his pocket.

Super Glue was invented by accident. The researcher was trying to make optical coating materials, and would test their properties by putting them between two prisms and shining light through them. When he tried the cyano-acrylate, he couldn't get the prisms apart.

No matter its size or thickness, no piece of paper can be folded in half more than seven times.

A car traveling at 80 kilometres per hour uses half its fuel to overcome wind resistance.

Knowledge is growing so fast that 90 per cent of what we will know in fifty years' time will be discovered in those fifty years.

According to an old English system of time, a moment is one and a half minutes.

The typewriter was invented in 1829 and the automatic dishwasher in 1889.

The wristwatch was invented in 1904 by Louis Cartier.

When glass breaks, the cracks move at speeds of up to 3,000 miles per hour.

By raising your legs slowly and laying on your back, you can't sink in quicksand.

Ten minutes of one hurricane contains enough energy to match the nuclear stockpiles of the world.

Most gemstones contain several elements. The exception? Diamond. It's all carbon.

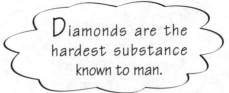

Diamonds are the hardest substance known to man.

Which of the fifty US states has never had an earthquake? North Dakota.

When hydrogen burns in the air, water is formed.

Sterling silver contains 7.5 per cent copper.

Cars were first made with ignition keys in 1949.

J.B. Dunlop was the first to put air into tyres.

Alexander Graham Bell, who invented the telephone, also set a world water-speed record of over 70 miles an hour at the age of seventy two.

It is energy-efficient to turn off a fluorescent light only if it will not be used again within an hour or more. This is because of the high voltage needed to turn it on, and the shortened life this high voltage causes.

Lake Baikal, in southern Siberia, is the deepest lake in the world.

The Earth's equatorial circumference (40,075 kilometres) is greater than its polar circumference (40,008 kilometres).

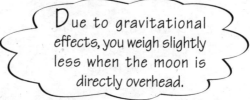

Due to gravitational effects, you weigh slightly less when the moon is directly overhead.

The Earth's average velocity orbiting the sun is 107,220 kilometres per hour.

There is a high and low tide because of our moon and the Sun.

The United States consumes 25 per cent of all the world's energy.

Flying from London to New York by Concord, due to the time zones crossed, you can arrive two hours before you leave.

There is enough fuel in a full tank of a Jumbo Jet to drive an average car four times around the world.

The surface speed record on the moon is 10.56 miles per hour. It was set with the lunar rover.

If you could drive to the sun—at 55 miles per hour—it would take about 193 years to reach.

The moon is one million times drier than the Gobi Desert.

Just twenty seconds worth of fuel remained when Apollo 11's lunar module landed on the moon.

A Boeing 707 uses 4,000 gallons of fuel in its take-off climb.

> The planet Saturn has a density lower than water. So, if placed on water, it would float.

Since 1959, more than 6,000 pieces of 'space junk' (abandoned rocket and satellite parts) have fallen out of the orbit. Many of these have hit the earth's surface.

It takes 70 per cent less energy to produce a ton of paper from recycled paper than from trees.

Every year in the US, 625 people are struck by lightning.

Hawaii is moving towards Japan 4 inches every year.

> The rocket engine has to supply its own oxygen so it can burn its fuel in outer space.

The North Atlantic gets 1 inch wider every year.

Oxygen is the most abundant element in the Earth's crust, waters and atmosphere (about 49.5 per cent)

A stroke of lightning discharges from 10 to 100 million volts and 30,000 amperes of electricity.

A bolt of lightning is about 54,000°F (30,000°C); six times hotter than the Sun.

Hydrogen is the most abundant element in the Universe (75 per cent).

The average distance between the Earth and the Moon is 238,857 miles (384,392 kilometres).

The moon is 27 per cent the size of the Earth.

The Earth weighs 6.6 sextillion tons, or 5.97 × 1,024 kilograms.

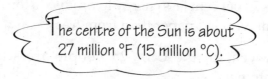

The centre of the Sun is about 27 million °F (15 million °C).

The highest temperature on Earth was 136°F (58°C) in Libya in 1922.

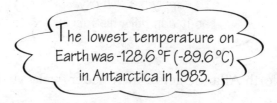

The lowest temperature on Earth was -128.6 °F (-89.6 °C) in Antarctica in 1983.

Sunlight can penetrate clean ocean water to a depth of 240 feet.

The average ocean floor is 12,000 feet.

The temperature can be determined by counting the number of cricket chirps in fourteen seconds and adding forty.

Houseflies have a lifespan of two weeks.

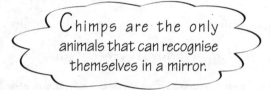

Chimps are the only animals that can recognise themselves in a mirror.

Starfish don't have brains.

The average person falls asleep in seven minutes.

Shrimps' hearts are in their heads.

Every time you lick a stamp, you are consuming one-tenth of a calorie.

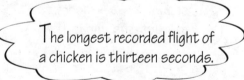

The longest recorded flight of a chicken is thirteen seconds.

Emus and kangaroos cannot walk backwards.

Cats have over 100 vocal sounds, while dogs only have about ten.

Porcupines float in water.

An ostrich's eye is bigger than its brain.

An iguana can stay under water for twenty eight minutes.

The common goldfish is the only animal that can see both infra-red and ultra-violet light.

It's impossible to sneeze with your eyes open.

The pupil of an octopus'si is rectangular.

Our eyes are always the same size from birth, but our nose and ears never stop growing.

The leg bones of a bat are so thin that no bat can walk.

Ants cannot chew their food; they move their jaws sideways, like scissors, to extract the juices from the food.

Hummingbirds are the only animals able to fly backwards.

A cat has thirty two muscles in each ear.

Tigers have striped skin, not just striped fur.

A cat's jaws cannot move sideways.

Armadillos get an average of 18.5 hours of sleep per day.

There are more beetles than any other kind of creatures in the world.

Armadillos can walk underwater.

Certain frogs can survive the experience of being frozen.

Only humans sleep on their backs.

The human brain is 80 per cent water.

Everyone's tongue print is different.

As an adult, you have more than 20 square feet of skin on your body—about the same square footage as a blanket for a queen-sized bed.

In your lifetime, you'll shed over 40 pounds of skin.

15 million blood cells are produced and destroyed in the human body every second.

Every minute, 30-40,000 dead skin cells fall from your body.

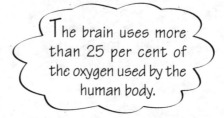

The brain uses more than 25 per cent of the oxygen used by the human body.

If your mouth was completely dry, you would not be able to distinguish the taste of anything.

Muscles are made up of bundles from about five in the eyelid to about 200 in the buttock muscle.

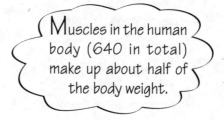

Muscles in the human body (640 in total) make up about half of the body weight.

The human body has enough fat to produce seven bars of soap.

The human head is a quarter of our total length at birth, but only an eighth of our total length by the time we reach adulthood.

Most people blink about 17,000 times a day.

Moths have no stomach.

Hummingbirds can't walk.

Sea otters have two coats of fur.

A starfish can turn its stomach inside out.

A zebra is white with black stripes.

The animal with the largest brain in relation to its body is the ant.

The largest eggs in the world are laid by a shark.

A crocodile's tongue is attached to the roof of its mouth.

Crocodiles swallow stones to help them dive deeper.

Giraffes are unable to cough.

Sharks are immune to cancer.

Despite the hump, a camel's spine is straight.

Cheetahs can accelerate from 0 to 70 kilometres per hour in three seconds.

A giraffe's neck contains the same number of vertebrae as a human.

The heart of a giraffe is two feet long, and can weigh as much as 24 pounds.

> On average, elephants sleep for about two hours per day.

Lobsters have blue blood.

Shark's teeth are literally as hard as steel.

A mosquito has forty seven teeth.

> Oxygen, carbon, hydrogen and nitrogen make up 90 per cent of the human body.

Seventy per cent of the dust in your home consists of shed human skin.

Fish are the only vertebrates that outnumber birds.

A cockroach can live for several weeks without its head.

The average human produces a quart of saliva a day—about 10,000 gallons in a lifetime.

Elephants have been known to remain standing after they die.

The embryos of tiger sharks fight each other while in their mother's womb, the survivor being the baby shark that is born.

Ants do not sleep.

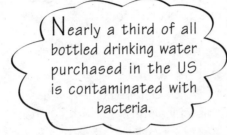

Nearly a third of all bottled drinking water purchased in the US is contaminated with bacteria.

Rats multiply so quickly that in eighteen months, two rats could have over 1 million descendants.

An Astronaut can be up to 2 inches taller returning from space. The cartilage disks in the spine expand in the absence of gravity.

The oldest known fossil is of a single-celled organism, blue-green algae, found in 3.2 billion year-old stones in South Africa.

The oldest multicellular fossils date from 700 million years ago.

The earliest cockroach fossils are about 280 million years old.

Healthy nails grow about 2 centimetres each year. Fingernails grow four times as fast as toenails.

20/20 vision means the eye can see normally at 20 feet. 20/15 is better; the eye can see at 20 feet what another eye sees at 15 feet.

The average person has 100,000 hairs on his/her head. Each hair grows about 5 inches (12.7 centimetres) every year.

SCIENCE THINK-TANK: QUOTES

Man will occasionally stumble over the truth, but usually manages to pick himself up, walk over or around it, and carry on.

On the sixth day, God created the platypus. And God said: let's see the evolutionists try and figure this one out.

> The goal of science and engineering is to build better mousetraps. The goal of nature is to build better mice.

I am not sure how clouds get formed. But the clouds know how to do it, and that is the important thing....

> The creator of the universe works in mysterious ways. But he uses a base.

Ten counting system likes round numbers.

—Scott Adams

Hypotheses, like professors, when they are seen not to work any longer in the laboratory, should disappear.
—Henry Edward Armstrong (1848-1937,
British chemist) in Sir Harold
Hartley, *Studies in the History of Chemistry* (1971)

Through the mythology of Einstein, the world blissfully regained the image of knowledge reduced to a formula.

—Roland Barthes, *Mythologies*, 1957

The history of science resembles a collection of ghosts remembering that once they too were gods.
—David Berlinsky, theoretical mathematician

A specialist knows more and more about less and less until eventually he knows everything about nothing.

A generalist knows less and less about more and more until eventually he knows nothing about everything.

Scientists are to journalists what rats are to scientists.
—Victor Cohn, medical writer, *Washington Post*

I believe that a scientist looking at nonscientific problems is just as dumb as the next guy.
—Richard P. Feynman

Science is a way of trying not to fool ourselves.
—Richard Feynman

That student is best taught who is told the least.
—*Quoted in D MacHale*, Comic Sections (Dublin 1993)

Scientific theories tell us what is possible; myths tell us what is desirable. Both are needed to guide proper action.
—John Maynard Smith (*Science and Myth*)

If I have seen further it is by standing on the shoulders of Giants.
—Isaac Newton (1642-1727) in: Letter to Robert Hooke, February 5, 1675/1676

In the sciences, we are now uniquely privileged to sit side by side with the giants on whose shoulders we stand.

—Gerald Holton

If I have not seen as far as others, it is because giants were standing on my shoulders.

—Hal Abelson

In computer science, we stand on each other's feet.

—Brian K. Reid

A dwarf standing on the shoulders of a giant may see farther than a giant himself.

—*The Anatomy of Melancholy* (1621-1651)

> Science is nothing but developed perception interpreted with intent.

Sense rounded out and minutely articulated.

—*George Santayana* (1863-1952) [US philosopher]

WERNER VON BRAUN

> Basic research is when I'm doing what I don't know I'm doing.

I have learned to use the word 'impossible' with the greatest caution.

The best computer is a man, and it's the only one that can be mass-produced by unskilled labour.

We can lick gravity, but sometimes the paperwork is overwhelming.

MURPHY'S LAWS

THE PRIME AXIOM: In any field of scientific endeavour, anything that can go wrong, will.

If the possibility exists of several things going wrong, the one that will go wrong is the one that will do the most damage.

Everything will go wrong at one time. That time is always when you least expect it.

If nothing can go wrong, something will.

Everything takes longer than you think.

Left to themselves, things always go from bad to worse.

Nature always sides with the hidden flaw.

Given the most inappropriate time for something to go wrong, that's when it will occur.

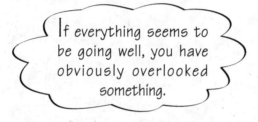

If in any problem you find yourself doing an immense amount of work, the answer can be obtained by simple inspection.

Never make anything simple and efficient when a way can be found to make it complex and wonderful.

If it doesn't fit, use a bigger hammer.

In an instrument or device characterised by a number of plus-or-minus errors, the total error will be the sum of all the errors adding in the same direction.

In any given calculation, the fault will never be placed if more than one person is involved. In any given discovery, the credit will never be properly placed if more than one person is involved.

> All warranty and guarantee clauses become invalid upon payment of the final invoice.

> Murphy's Law: 'If there are two or more ways to do something, and one of those ways can result in a catastrophe, then someone will do it.'

EINSTEIN BYTES

In the past it never occurred to me that every casual remark of mine would be snatched up and recorded. Otherwise I would have crept further into my shell.
—Einstein to his biographer Carl Seelig (October 25, 1953)

WHY EINSTEIN IS FAMOUS

When a blind beetle crawls over the surface of a curved branch, it doesn't notice that the track it has covered is indeed curved. I was lucky enough to notice what the beetle didn't notice.

—Einstein, in answer to his son Eduard's question
why he is so famous, 1922

With fame, I become more and
more stupid, which of course is
a very common phenomenon.
—Albert Einstein (to Heinrich
Zanger, Dec 1919)

Just as with the man in the fairy tale who turned everything he touched into gold, with me everything is turned into newspaper clamour.

—Albert Einstein (to Max Born, Sep 9, 1920)

If we knew what it was we were doing, it would not be called research, would it?

—Albert Einstein

Gravitation cannot be
held responsible for people
falling in love.
—Albert Einstein

The wireless telegraph is not difficult to understand. The ordinary telegraph is like a very long cat. You pull the tail in New York, and it meows in Los Angeles. The wireless is the same, only without the cat.

—Albert Einstein

> When asked how World War III would be fought, Einstein replied that he didn't know. But he knew how World War IV would be fought: With sticks and stones!

Put your hand on a hot stove for a minute, and it seems like an hour. Sit with a pretty girl for an hour, and it seems like a minute. THAT'S relativity.

Sometimes one pays most for the things one gets for nothing.

—Einstein, Albert (1879-1955)* Science without religion is lame, religion without science is blind.

If I would be a young man again and had to decide how to make my living, I would not try to become a scientist or scholar or teacher. I would rather choose to be a plumber or a peddler in the hope to find that modest degree of independence still available under present circumstances.

—Albert Einstein, *The Reporter*, November 18, 1954

God does not play dice with the universe.

—Einstein

Who are you to tell God what to do?

—Bohr

God not only plays dice, but sometimes throws them where they cannot be seen.

—Hawking

God plays dice with the universe,
but they're loaded dice.
—Joseph Ford, Physicist

It seems certain that Einstein was doubly wrong when he said 'God does not play dice.' Consideration of particle emission from black holes would seem to suggest that God not only plays dice but also sometimes throws them where they cannot be seen.

—Dr Stephen W. Hawking, *NATURE*, 1975

God does not play dice with the universe; He plays an ineffable game of His own devising, which might be compared, from the perspective of the players, (i.e. everybody), to being involved in an obscure and complex version of poker in a pitch-dark room, with blank cards, for infinite stakes, with a dealer who won't tell you the rules, and who smiles all the time.

—*Good Omens* by Neil Gaiman and Terry Pratchett

Two things are infinite: the universe and human stupidity; and I'm not sure about the universe.

—Albert Einstein

The most incomprehensible thing about the universe is that it is comprehensible.'

—Albert Einstein

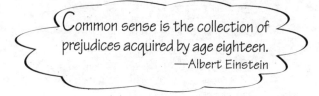

Common sense is the collection of prejudices acquired by age eighteen.
—Albert Einstein

Nothing will benefit human health and increase the chances for survival of life on Earth as much as the evolution to a vegetarian diet. You do not really understand something unless you can explain it to your grandmother.

—Albert Einstein

I want to know God's thoughts; the rest are details.

Anyone who has never made a mistake has never tried anything new.

Science is a wonderful thing if one does not have to earn one's living at it.

The secret to creativity is knowing how to hide your sources.

One had to cram all this stuff into one's mind for the examinations.

God does not care about our mathematical difficulties. He integrates empirically.

> Whether one liked it or not, this coercion had such a deterring effect on me that after I had passed the final examination, I found the consideration of any scientific problems distasteful to me for an entire year.

One of the strongest motives that lead men to art and science is escape from everyday life with its painful crudity and hopeless dreariness, from the fetters of one's own ever-shifting desires.

> A finely tempered nature longs to escape from the personal life into the world of objective perception and thought.

I never thought that others would take them so much more seriously then I did.
—Albert Einstein about his theories.

It is a miracle that curiosity survives formal education.
—Albert Einstein

I tried to imagine the easiest way God could have done it.

—Albert Einstein

I believe that every true theorist is a kind of tamed metaphysicist, no matter how pure a 'positivist' he may fancy himself to be.

—Albert Einstein

The dog is very smart. He feels sorry for me because I receive so much mail; that's why he tries to bite the mailman.

—Albert Einstein, regarding his dog Chico

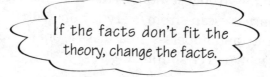

If the facts don't fit the theory, change the facts.

DID YOU KNOW?

Glass is made from sand.

Glass, which looks like a solid, is actually a very slow moving liquid.

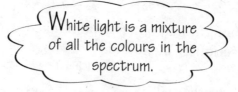

White light is a mixture of all the colours in the spectrum.

Some forms of primitive life can survive anywhere water is found, even in boiling water or ice.

The sound of a whip cracking is actually a mini sonic boom that occurs when the tip of the whip breaks the sound barrier.

Eleanor Rosevelt received a telegram from the 1939 World's Fair in New York that used only the power from electric eels.

Using nanotechnology, a microscopic guitar with strings has been made. It is no larger than a blood cell.

During a four year period, inventor Thomas Edison registered almost 300 patents.

John Logie Baird made the first television in 1924 using cardboard, scrap wood, needles, string and other materials.

More than a thousand new insects are discovered every year.

A cross between a goat and a sheep is called a 'geep'.

Thomas Edison was afraid of the dark.

Sir Isaac Newton invented the cat flap.

English chemist John Walker never patented his invention of matches because he felt such an important tool should be public property.

Honey is sometimes used in antifreeze mixtures and in the centre of golf balls.

The first stethoscope was made in 1816 with a roll of paper.

Cat urine glows under black light.

Hot water freezes more quickly than cold water.

The Eiffel Tower always leans away from the sun because heat makes the metal expand.

PATENT MANIA

Patent no. GB2272154 is for a ladder to enable spiders to climb out of a bath. The ladder comprises a thin, flexible strip of latex rubber that follows the inner contours of the bath. A suction pad on the ladder is attached to the top of the bath.

Patent no. GB2060081 is for a horse-powered minibus. The horse walks along a conveyor belt in the middle of the bus. This drives the wheels via a gearbox. A thermometer under the horse's collar is connected to the vehicle instrument panel. The driver can signal to the horse using a handle, which brings a mop into contact with the horse.

Patent no. GB2172200 is for an umbrella for wearing on the head. The support frame is designed not to mess up the wearer's hair.

Patent no. US4233942 is for a device for protecting the ears of a long-haired dog from becoming soiled by food while it is eating. A tube contains each of the dog's ears. The tubes are held away from the dog's mouth and food while it eats.

Patent no. WO9701384 is for a leash for walking an imaginary pet. It has a preformed shape and supports a simulated pet harness and collar. A micro loudspeaker in the collar is connected to an integrated circuit in the handle, to produce a variety of barks and growls.

Patent no. GB1453920 is for rolled-up fire curtains at roof level on a skyscraper. When a fire starts, the curtains are released to cover the building and suffocate the fire.

Patent no. US5971829 is for a motorised ice-cream cone. The cone spins while you lick the ice cream.

Patent no. US2760763 is for an egg beater that beats the egg within its shell.

Patent no. US6637447 is for the 'Beerbrella'. This is a tiny umbrella that clips onto a beer bottle, keeping the sun off the beverage.

Patent no. WO98/21939 is for deer ears. To use, simply place the deer ears on your head and swivel your new ears in the direction you would like to hear.

Patent no. US3150831 is for a birthday cake candle extinguisher.

Patent no. US5713081 is for three-legged pantyhose. When there is a run in the stocking, you simply rotate your leg into the spare hose. The damaged hose is then tucked into a pocket in the crotch of the pantyhose.

Patent no. US5719656 is for earless eyewear. Stick the self-adhesive magnets on to each side of your head. The eyewear frames contain internal magnets that hold on to the magnets on your temples.

Patent no. US4022227 is for a three-way comb-over to cover a bald head. Just let your hair grow long at the sides, then divide it into three sections and comb it over your bald head one section at a time.

Patent no. US4872422 is for a pet petter. This is an electronic device consisting of an eye that spots your pet and signals the electronic motors to activate the petting arm. The arm is tipped with a human-like hand for added realism.

Patent no. USD342712 is for a frame that clamps around your pet's waist and supports a clear plastic tent-like structure that keeps your pet dry in the rain. There are air holes in the tent.

Patent no. US6557994 is for a way to hang eyeglasses on your face. You use body piercing studs. Pierce your eyebrows and hang your glasses from the studs. There is also a design that works with a nose bridge stud.

Patent no. US4825469 is for a fully inflatable motorcycle suit. When the rider falls off the bike, the suit swells with compressed gas until it covers the head, arms, torso and legs, protecting the rider from damage.

Patent no. US3842343 is for mud flaps to keep mud from flying up the back of your shoes.

Patent no. US6704666 is for the 'Speak & Swing', which is a motorised golf club selection system. You simply speak to your golf bag, telling it which club you want, and the club automatically pops up.

Patent no. US6600372 is for the 'Spitting Duck'. This device fits most toilets and instead of using toilet paper, you lift the duck's bill and a strategically placed nozzle will spray your bottom with the cleaning formula.

Patent no US5372954 is for the 'Wig Flipper'. A wig is placed on a large spring and attached to a small cap.

The wig and spring are then compressed, locked on to the cap and placed on your head. When you push the spring release button, the hairpiece will jump into the air.

Patent no. US5352633 is for the 'Arm Mitten', which the driver of a car wears on one arm. This protects the arm from sunburn when the elbow rests on the window ledge.

Patent no. US5848443 is for the 'Travel Relief'. This is a padded toilet for use while driving. It even flushes.

Patent no. US5375340 is for 'Cool Shoes', which are air-conditioned shoes that have a mini-network of heat exchange coils built into the heels. With each step, the wearer activates the compressor chamber, which forces cool air up into the shoe via a rubber bladder in the sole.

SCIENCE AND TECH

> The search engine Google got its name from the word 'googol', which refers to the number one with a hundred zeros after it.

Another name for a Microsoft Windows tutorial is 'Crash Course'!

Medical research has found substances in mistletoe that can slow down tumour growth.

Microsoft made $16,005 in revenue in its first year of operation.

> There are more than 1,000 chemicals in a cup of coffee; of these, only twenty six have been tested ,and half of them caused cancer in rats.

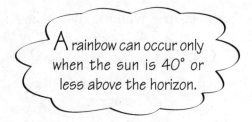

A rainbow can occur only
when the sun is 40° or
less above the horizon.

Britney Spears, Anna Kournikova, Osama bin Laden,
Avril Lavigne, Michelangelo and Tonya Harding
have all had computer viruses named after them.

WORLD OF SCIENCE

The best working light-bulb a long time ago was a
thread of sheep's wool coated with carbon.

A bolt of lightning can strike the earth with a force as
great as 100 million volts.

A cubic mile of fog is made up of less than a gallon of
water.

A full moon always rises at sunset.

A full moon is nine times brighter than a half moon.

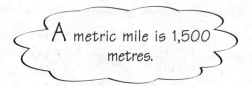

A metric mile is 1,500
metres.

A pedometer measures walking distance.

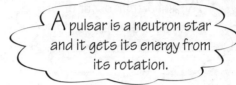

A pulsar is a neutron star and it gets its energy from its rotation.

The shell constitutes 12 per cent of an egg's weight.

A standard grave is 7'8 x 3'2 x 6'.

A wind with a speed of 74 miles or more is designated a hurricane.

An iceberg contains more heat than a match.

An inch of snow falling evenly on one acre of ground is equivalent to about 2,715 gallons of water.

Approximately 98 per cent of software in China is pirated.

At room temperature, the average air molecule travels at the speed of a rifle bullet.

Bacteria, the tiniest free-living cells, are so small that a single drop of liquid contains as many as 50 million of them.

Bamboo (the world's tallest grass) can grow up to 90 centimetres in a day.

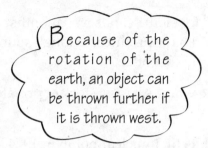

Because of the rotation of the earth, an object can be thrown further if it is thrown west.

By weight, the sun is 70 per cent hydrogen, 28 per cent helium, 1.5 per cent carbon, nitrogen and oxygen, and 0.5 per cent all other elements.

DuPont is the world's largest chemical company.

Earth is travelling through space at 660,000 miles per hour.

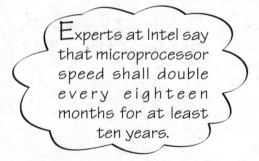

Experts at Intel say that microprocessor speed shall double every eighteen months for at least ten years.

Gold was the first metal to be discovered.

Hydrogen is the most common atom in the universe.

If you attempted to count the stars in a galaxy at a rate of one every second, it would take around 3,000 years to count them all.

If you yelled for eight years, seven months and six days, you would have produced enough sound energy to heat one cup of coffee.

India has the world's largest stock of privately hoarded gold.

India tested its first nuclear bomb in 1974.

Iron nails cannot be used in oak because the acid in the wood corrodes them.

Japan's currency is the most difficult to counterfeit.

Mercury is the only metal that is liquid at room temperature.

Moisture, not air, causes superglue to dry.

Rene Descartes came up with the theory of co-ordinate geometry by looking at a fly walk across a tiled ceiling.

Robots in Japan pay union dues.

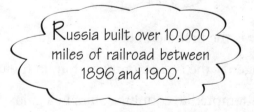

Russia built over 10,000 miles of railroad between 1896 and 1900.

Stainless steel was discovered by accident in 1913.

Sunbeams that shine down through clouds are called crepuscular rays.

The 'Big Bang' is said to have created the universe.

The average life of a nuclear plant is forty years.

The Boeing 737 jet is nicknamed 'Fat Albert'.

The Boeing 747 has been in commercial service since 1970.

The colour black is produced by the complete absorption of light rays.

The company Kodak is the largest user of silver.

The 111th element is known as Unnilenilenium.

The process of splitting atoms is called fission.

The smallest unit of time is the yoctosecond.

The tail section of an airplane gives the bumpiest ride.

The speed of sound must be exceeded to produce a sonic boom.

The total quantity of energy in the universe is constant.

The two hottest months at the equator are March and September.

The Venus flytrap can eat a whole cheeseburger.

Three stars make up Orion's belt.

Twenty years make up a vicennial period.

You are most likely to lose your hearing than any of the other senses if you are hit by lightning.

Galaxy is derived from the ancient Greek word for milk.

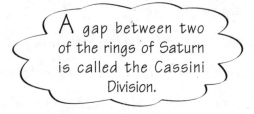

A gap between two of the rings of Saturn is called the Cassini Division.

Proxima Centauri is the nearby star of the earth other than the sun.

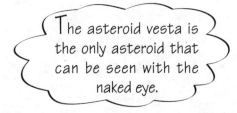

The asteroid vesta is the only asteroid that can be seen with the naked eye.

Sirius is the brightest star in the night sky.

Charon is the name of Pluto's only moon.

The everyday name for plants that have the scientific classification Graminaese is Grasses.

Morphology is the study of shape of plants and animals.

Friday is named after the Scandinavian goddess of love Frigga.

The month of March is named after the Roman God of war.

September is not the seventh month (Septem) but the ninth.

Calendar comes from Kalendae or Calendae, the first day of each month in the ancient Roman calendar.

The Chinese calendar had years counted from the accession of the emperor until 1911 AD.

Thursday is named after the Norse god of thunder.

The 18th century French Chemist Antoine Lavoisier was guillotined during the French Revolution.

'W' is the single letter chemical symbol for Tungsten.

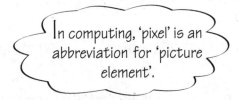

In computing, 'pixel' is an abbreviation for 'picture element'.

The software package of Microsoft Excel is spreadsheet.

Dinosaur means 'Terrible Lizard.'

Coprolites is the scientific name for fossilized dinosaur.

Brontosaurus dinosaur means 'Three horned face'.

Werner Heisenberg, the German scientist is famous for his 'uncertainty principle'.

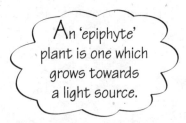

An 'epiphyte' plant is one which grows towards a light source.

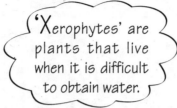

'Xerophytes' are plants that live when it is difficult to obtain water.

The nares is the correct scientific term for the nostrils.

The 'oil of vitriol' is sulphuric acid.

Star clusters refer to Messier numbers.

The island of Langerhans is found in the ear.

Thomas Edison was known as 'The Wizard of Menlo Park.'

Nylon was invented by Wallace Carothers.

George Eastman invented the Kodak Camera.

William Semple invented chewing gum in 1869 to be a means of exercising the face.

An early form of calculating machine was Napier's Bones.

In Geometry, you can find a phenomenon known as the 'Witch of Agnesi'.

Brain cells are the only cells that never re-grow.

> The medical condition lateral epicondylitis is commonly known as 'Tennis elbow'.

The drug Digitalis is obtained from the plant foxglove.

T. H. Laennec invented the stethoscope in 1816.

The common name for the disease Varicella is 'chicken pox.'

The armpit is called the axilla.

Ebola, a viral disease takes its name from a river in the Republic of Congo.

Aspirin was the first painkiller to be patented in 1899.

Red colour light has the highest frequency.

> A cesium atom is an atomic clock that beats 9,192,631,770 times a second.

A device invented as a primitive steam engine by the Greek engineer Hero, about the time of the birth of Christ, is used today as a rotating lawn sprinkler.

A fully loaded supertanker travelling at normal speed takes at least twenty minutes to stop.

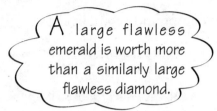

A large flawless emerald is worth more than a similarly large flawless diamond.

A manned rocket can reach the moon in less time than it took a stagecoach to travel the length of England.

A neutron star has such a powerful gravitational pull that it can spin on its axis in one-thirtieth of a second without tearing itself apart.

A silicon chip a quarter-inch square has the capacity of the original 1949 ENIAC computer, which occupied a city block.

A syzygy occurs when three astronomical bodies line up.

About seven million cars are junked each year in the US.

According to the Gemological Institute of America, up until 1869 India was the only source for diamonds in the world.

All organic compounds contain carbons.

All snow crystals are hexagonal.

All the gold produced in the past 500 years, if melted, could be compressed into a 50-foot cube.

All the stars in our galaxy, the Milky Way, revolve around the centre of the galaxy every 200 million years.

All totalled, the sunlight that strikes earth at any given moment weighs as much as an ocean liner.

Almost all the helium that exists in the world today is from natural-gas wells in the United States.

An enneahedron is solid with nine faces.

Any free-moving liquid in outer space will form itself into a sphere because of its surface tension.

Astronomers classify stars by their spectra.

At any given time, there are 1,800 thunderstorms in progress over the earth's atmosphere.

Back in the mid to late 80s, an IBM-compatible computer wasn't considered hundred per cent

compatible unless it could run Microsoft's Flight
Simulator.

Carolyn Shoemaker has
discovered thirty two
comets and approximately
300 asteroids.

Clouds fly higher during the day than the night.

It takes one fifteen to twenty year-old tree to produce
700 paper grocery bags.

Lab tests can detect traces of alcohol in urine six to
twelve hours after a person has stopped drinking.

Life on earth probably developed in an oxygen-free
atmosphere. Even today there are microorganisms
that can live only in the absence of oxygen.

Man releases over a billion
tons of pollutants into
the earth's atmosphere
every year.

Methane gas can often be seen bubbling up from the
bottom of ponds. It is produced by the decomposition
of dead plants and animals in the mud.

One ragweed plant can release as many as one billion
grains of pollen.

Orchids are grown from seeds so small that it would take 30,000 to weigh as much as one grain of wheat.

South Africa produces two-thirds of the world's gold.

Stars come in different colours; hot stars give off blue light and the cooler stars give off red light.

The ashes of the metal Magnesium are heavier than the metal itself.

The bark of a redwood tree is fireproof. Fires that occur in a redwood forest take place inside the trees.

The billionth digit of PI is nine.

The US Bureau of Standards says that the electron is the fastest thing in the world.

The CN Tower, in Toronto, is the tallest free-standing structure in the world.

The colour of diamond dust is black.

The he condensed water vapour left by jets in the sky is called a contrail.

The densest substance on earth is the metal osmium.

The first product Motorola started to develop was a record player for automobiles. At that time the most well-known player in the market was the Victrola, so they called themselves Motorola.

The leaves of the Victorian water lily are sometimes over 6 feet in diameter.

The metal instrument used in shoe stores to measure feet is called the Brannock device.

The radio-active substance, Americanium-241 is used in many smoke detectors.

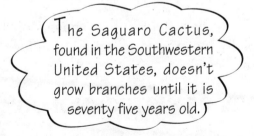

The Saguaro Cactus, found in the Southwestern United States, doesn't grow branches until it is seventy five years old.

The strength of early lasers was measured in Gillettes, the number of blue razor blades a given beam could puncture.

The US standard railroad gauge (distance between rails) is 4 feet 8.5 inches.

There are 5 tillion trillion atoms in one pound of iron.

Three astronauts manned each Apollo flight.

When CBS broadcast the first television show in colour, no one other than CBS owned a colour television set.

Nanotechnology works in an almost unimaginably small dimension, using the nanometre, a billionth of a metre, as a basic measurement.

Biotechnology is technology based on biology, especially when used in agriculture, food science, and medicine.

HISTORY OF BIOTECHNOLOGY

8000 BC: Collecting of seeds for replanting. Evidence that Babylonians, Egyptians and Romans used selective breeding practices to improve livestock.

6000BC: Brewing beer, fermenting wine, baking bread with the help of yeast.

4000BC: Chinese made yoghurt and cheese with lactic-acid-producing bacteria.

1500AD: Plant collecting around the world.

1880AD: Microorganisms discovered.

1856AD: Gregor Mendel started recombinant plant genetics.

1980AD: Modern biotech with recombinant DNA, mostly on best studied E. coli bacteria to produce insulin and other medicines, in human form (rather than before used animal insulins, to which about 5 per cent of diabetics are allergic).

ELECTRICITY FUN FACTS

Electric current is measured in amperes (amps).

Electric potential energy is measured in volts.

Two positive charges repel each other, as do two negative charges. Opposite charges on the other hand attract each other.

When an electric charge builds up on the surface of an object it creates static electricity. You have probably experienced static electricity in the form of a small electric shock, which is what happens when the electric charge is quickly neutralized by an opposite charge.

Electric eels can produce strong electric shocks of around 500 volts for both self-defence and hunting.

Electric circuits can contain parts such as switches, transformers and resistors.

A common way to produce electricity is by hydropower, a process that generates electricity by using water to spin turbines attached to generators.

The world's biggest source of energy for producing electricity comes from coal. The burning of coal in furnaces heats boiler water until it becomes steam which then spins turbines attached to generators.

Lightning is a discharge of electricity in the atmosphere. Lightning bolts can travel at around 210,000 kilo metres per hour (130,000 miles per hour), while reaching nearly 30,000 °C (54,000 °F) in temperature.

Electricity plays a role in the way your heart beats. Muscle cells in the heart are contracted by electricity going through the heart.

Electrocardiogram (ECG) machines used in hospitals measure the electricity going through someone's heart; when the person is healthy it usually shows a line moving across a screen with regular spikes as the heart beats.

You may have heard of direct current (DC) and alternating current (AC). The difference between the two is in the way the electrons flow. In DC electrons move in a single direction while in AC they change directions, switching between backwards and forwards. The electricity used in your home is AC while DC comes from sources that include batteries.

Back in the 1880s, there was even a 'war of currents' between Thomas Edison (who helped invent DC) and Nikola Tesla (who helped invent AC). Both wanted their system to be used, with AC eventually winning due to the fact that it is safer and can be used over longer distances.

American Benjamin Franklin carried out extensive electricity research in the 18th century, inventing the lightning rod amongst his many discoveries. Lightning rods protect buildings in the event of lightning by conducting lightning strikes through a grounded wire.

RECYCLING FACTS: WATER

A running faucet wastes 2.5 gallons of water each minute.

A dishwasher uses 11 gallons of water per use.

75 per cent of all water used in the household is used in the bathroom.

A toilet made in 1992 or earlier uses up to 60 per cent more water per flush than newer high efficiency toilets.

Turning the tap off while brushing your teeth in the morning and before bedtimes can save up to 8 gallons per day. This is 240 gallons saved per month.

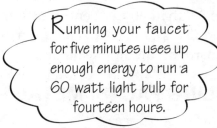

Running your faucet for five minutes uses up enough energy to run a 60 watt light bulb for fourteen hours.

A full bath tub uses 70 gallons of water. A 5 minute shower only uses 10-25 gallons.

RECYCLING FACTS: PAPER

Recycling 1 ton of paper saves seventeen mature trees, 7,000 gallons of water, 3 cubic yards of landfill space, 2 barrels of oil, and 4,000 kilowatt hours of electricity. This is enough energy to power the average American home for 5 months.

The process of recycling paper instead of making it from new materials causes 74 per cent less air pollution and uses 50 per cent less water.

Manufacturing recycled paper uses 60 per cent of the energy needed to make paper from new materials.

Over 73 per cent of all newspapers are recovered for recycling. About 33 per cent of this is used to make newsprint the rest is used to make paperboard, tissue, or insulation.

A little more than 48 per cent of all office paper is recycled. This is used to make writing papers, paperboard, tissue, and insulation.

RECYCLING FACTS: METAL

Recycling steel and tin cans saves 74 per cent of the energy used to make them.

Americans throw away enough aluminum every month to rebuild an entire commercial air fleet.

Americans throw out enough iron and steel to continuously supply all the automakers in the entire nation.

A steel mill using recycled scrap reduces water pollution, air pollution, and mining waste by about 70 per cent.

When you throw away an aluminum can, you waste as much energy as if you'd filled the can half full of gasoline and poured it into the ground.

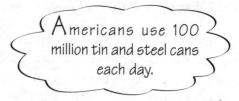

Americans use 100 million tin and steel cans each day.

Recycling one aluminum can saves enough energy to run a 100 watt light bulb for twenty hours, a computer for three hours and a TV for two hours!

RECYCLING FACTS: PLASTIC

Enough plastic is produced in the United States each year to shrink wrap Texas.

In 1998 Americans used 2 billion pounds of HDPE to make plastic bottles for household products. That's the equivalent weight of 90,000 Honda Civics.

Approximately 88 per cent of the energy is saved when plastic is made from plastic rather than from the raw materials of gas and oil.

Enough plastic bottles are thrown away in the United States each year to circle the Earth four times.

DINOSAUR FACTS

The word was coined by English paleontologist Richard Owen in 1842 and was meant to refer to Dinosaurs' impressive size rather than their scary appearance.

Dinosaurs ruled the Earth for over 160 million years, from the Triassic period around 230 million years ago through the Jurassic period and until the end of the Cretaceous period around 65 million years ago.

The time period from 250 million years ago until around 65 million years ago is known as the Mesozoic Era. It is often referred to as the Age of the Dinosaurs because most dinosaurs developed and became extinct during this time.

Scientists believe that the event leading to the extinction may have been a massive asteroid impact or huge volcanic activity. Events such as these could have blocked out sunlight and significantly changed the Earth's ecology.

The first dinosaur to be formally named was the Megalosaurus, back in 1824.

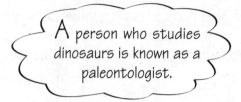

A person who studies dinosaurs is known as a paleontologist.

Rather than being carnivores (meat eaters), the largest dinosaurs such as the Brachiosaurus and Apatosaurus were actually herbivores (plant eaters).

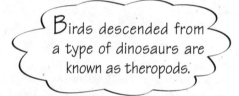

Birds descended from a type of dinosaurs are known as theropods.

MORE FACTS

The name *noobinator* means 'egg thief.'

A dinosaur that is called Velociraptor means 'fast thief.'

Fossilized dinosaur eggs have been found as recently as 1991 in China.

The scary creatures were made even more popular by the movie, *Jurassic Park*.

The animal living today thought to have evolved from the last of the theropoddinosaurs from the Jurassic period is the Bird.

The fierce predator and close relative of the Velociraptor that could grow up to 7 metres (20 feet) in length and weighed almost a ton was the Utahraptor.

Triceratops was a herbivore, feeding on plants and shrubbery with his sharp beak, had three horns – one on its snout and two more above the eyes.

Megalosaurus was the first dinosaur, thought to be a large meat-eater was 9 metres (30 feet) tall and weighed about 1 ton. It was discovered in 1676 when a jawbone and teeth were unearthed in Oxford, England.

Stegosaurus means 'covered lizard.'

The Argentinosaurus is believed to have been the largest animal to ever walk the earth, reaching lengths of up to 150 feet and weighing as much as 110 tons.

GOLD IN OCEANS

It is estimated by scientists that the oceans on Earth contain about 20 tons of gold. This gold, however, exists in small non-extractable amounts.

THE AMAZING HUMAN BODY

Did you know that a baby's weight is increased about five million times on the 238 days before it is born? It also triples within the baby's first year as it gains about 1 1/2 to 2 pounds a month.

WEIRD RAIN FALLING

There are parts in the Chilean Atacama Desert where rain has never fallen, making it one of the driest places on Earth. Yet, in the Amazon rainforest, where 30,000 different plants and 2,500 types of trees thrive, 10 feet of rain falls every year. One-third of the world's vegetation is grown in the Amazon.

PINK DOLPHINS

There is a dolphin that lives in the Amazon river, also known as Boto, that is pink in colour. It is the only fresh water dolphin in South America, where they see it as a mythical creature revered for its ability to change into human form.

INCAS BRAIN SURGERY

Using basic tools the Incas successfully performed brain surgery about 1,000 years ago. They operated without anesthesia by drilling holes in the skull of the patient. Apparently, by the amount of skulls that have been found with these trepanation holes, it was very common.

THE BIG UNIVERSE

It is not known how big the universe is, but it is so vast that astronomers measure it in light years. A light year is how fast light travels in a year, and light is the fastest thing in the universe. Light travels at 299,742,458 metres per second, or 186,000 miles per second.

The Sumerians were not the first to realise that certain points of light in the sky moved while others stayed still. But they were the first to write on clay tablets and the first to be noted in history.

While the Greeks were best at using the imagination to arrive at explanations that were theoretical and not dependent only on mythology, the Sumerians were best at predicting lunar eclipses, organising a calendar and measuring the exact movements of planets.

The Greeks gave us natural philosophers who gathered together and made astronomical observations using a sundial. Thales, Anassimene and Anassimandro drew nautical charts, hypothesized on Earth's structure and the laws under which the planets and stars moved.

Then in the 6th century BC came the Pythagoras school, in which the thought came about that the Earth must be spherical and that the movements of stars follow perfect number laws. Aristotle's fame and prestige contributed to the belief that all the planets revolved around the Earth due to the love of the 'divine immobile motor'.

Even though we know those beliefs were erroneous, it was quite an accomplishment to come up with such reasonings at a time when all they had was their eyes and minds to arrive at answers to our surroundings and existence.

But not long after these assumptions became accepted theories, an astronomer came along who actually chose to measure. Aristarch de Samo (310-330 BC) would be the first true astronomer in history as he chose logical convictions that were correct. He not only used logic, but he also utilised mathematical instruments to investigate the cosmos.

Samo was the first to deduct that the Earth and planets revolve around an immobile sun and also that the stars are found at huge distances from Earth. He calculated the distances from the Earth to the Sun and Moon using logical mathematical means. Even though his numbers were slightly mistaken due to the measurements done by eye that tend to be inaccurate, he tried to approach his problem with logic and mathematics. This was a great accomplishment for a time when philosophical means were more the norm with great scholars.

Another great scientist of the time was Eratostene de Cirene (276 - 194 BC) who, using a simple mathematical calculation, determined the dimensions of the Earth with extreme accuracy. His value measured at 39,400 kilometres while the real value we know today is 40,009 kilometres.

Many more scientists and astronomers were using mathematics and logic to come up with answers to the major questions about Earth, the planets and stars. Unfortunately, many still chose to believe in Aristotle's great thesis because it was simpler to accept. So not much happened in the way of new astronomical discoveries for about 300 years.

A great sight in the sky these days, Jupiter is the largest planet in the solar system and fifth from the Sun. It was named after the king of the Roman Gods.

Jupiter is approximately 484 million miles from the Sun
    and takes almost twelve years to complete its orbit
    around it. Jupiter rotates very fast so its day is only
    ten hours long. Due to this fast rotation, the planet
    is also not entirely spherical; it has a trivial bulge
    around the middle since the fastest spin occurs at
    the equator. Because of this, Jupiter has a slight oval
    profile.

The planet is so big that you could fit 1,300 Earths inside of it. Jupiter has a total of forty nine official moons and fourteen unofficial ones.

Of these sixty three moons, there are four that are the most widely known. These largest moons orbiting Jupiter are Lo, Europa, Ganymede and Callisto.

These large moons are all interesting worlds in their
    own right. Astrobiologists think that Europa
    could even have the potential for a habitable zone.
    Some life forms have been found thriving near

underground volcanoes and under many other extreme conditions on Earth. Europa may be very similar to those extreme locations on Earth, so life could have developed there as well.

Jupiter is a gaseous planet, its atmosphere is made up of hydrogen and helium with small traces of ammonia, rock, water and methane. It is believed to have a solid rock core as big as 18 Earth masses; this core can get as hot as 20,000 °F, while the cloud-top temperature is a very cold -170 °F.

Atoms one the building blocks of matter. The Greeks named the atom, as the word means indivisible, when they concluded that matter could be broken down into small particles that could not be further divided.

However, today we know that to be untrue, as the atom has been split, giving us nuclear fission—such as occurs in a nuclear explosion. Also, we know that atoms contain a nucleus with smaller particles called protons, electrons and neutrons. Furthermore, these smaller particles can also be broken down into even smaller ones.

The first controlled atom splitting, or nuclear fission, was done by Enrico Fermi in 1942 at the University Chicago. But many physicists and chemists were already aware of the weapon's potential in nuclear fusion in the 1930s. It was a fairly unknown scientist called Leo Szilard who insisted that Einstein send the famous letter to President Roosevelt urging him to form what became known as the Manhattan Project, which made possible the advent of nuclear weapons.

An atom consists of a nucleus that is made up of protons with a positive charge and neutrons, which are neutral. Spinning very fast around the nucleus are the smaller and lighter negatively charged electrons. Atoms have the same number of electrons and protons, which make them electrically neutral.

The protons are held together in the nucleus by a very powerful force called the nuclear force, as they naturally repel each other electrically.

Each chemical element's atoms have a different nuclei consisting of a different proton and neutron number. The atoms of heavy elements have large numbers of protons and neutrons.

We may never have flying cars, but the future is here. From creating fully functioning artificial leaves to hacking the human brain, science made a lot of breakthroughs this year.

Our lungs are known to be the lightest of all organs in the body.

Turritopsisnutricula is a genus of jelly fish which is also regarded as the immortal jelly fish. This is because these species have the ability to transform back into juvenile form once they mate after becoming sexually mature.

Nothing can be quieter than space. Even if a star explodes, you would hear nothing. No air molecules, no vibration thus, no sound.

Some chameleons have tongues which are longer than their body.

'One' happens to be the only number whose letters are according to the reverse alphabetical order. While, 'forty', has letters in the alphabetical order.

We all know that light takes 8 minutes to reach the earth. But the same light took a whopping 30,000 years to make it to the sun's surface from its core!

A blue whale's tongue is as heavy as an adult elephant and even bigger than a taxi cab.

On an average, man is able to produce enough spit to fill a swimming pool.

Buy an electric eel found in South America and reduce your electricity bills. This creature can produce 600 volts; voltage enough to paralyze a horse.

The sound produced by the blue whale counts up to about 188 decibels. No wonder, it can be heard even from 853 kilometres.

How much does the average man sleep in his entire lifetime? The armadillo spends about 80 per cent of its life in sleeping.

If you bring two similar metals (having clean and flat surfaces) together, they would fuse naturally, only when the process is performed in vacuum. This is known as cold welding.

If you want to grow taller, say by 2 inches, take a trip to space. As there is no gravity, the spine becomes free to elongate up to 2 inches. The same happens when we are sleeping, except that the spine stretches up to 1 or 2 centimetres then.

In ancient times, leeches were used as weather forecasters. When they were kept in water jars, they seemed to stay at the bottom during calm weather. It so happened that when a storm approached, these creatures rose quickly to the top, and descended as the storm passed.

More than our own cells in our body, there are microbial cells.

Liver is the only organ which has the capability of regenerating itself.

The planet Mercury has a day that is twice as long as its year.

The Pyramid of Giza is the result of an accumulation of 2.5 million blocks.

Pumice is the only known rock which can float on water.

Rabbits and parrots can see behind themselves without even moving their heads!

A hippopotamus may seem huge but it can still run faster than a man.

Even if an analog clock is broken, it shows the correct time twice a day.

Sneezing with your eyes open is impossible.

The trickiest tongue twister in the English language is apparently 'Sixth sick sheik's sixth sheep's sick'. Give it a try and see for yourself.

FUN OCEAN FACTS

Around 70 per cent of the Earth's surface is covered by oceans.

The world's oceans contain enough water to fill a cube with edges over 1000 kilometres (621 miles) in length.

Ocean tides are caused by the Earth rotating while the Moon and Sun's gravitational pull acts on ocean water.

While there are hundreds of thousands of known marine life forms, there are many that are yet to be discovered. Some scientists suggest that there could actually be millions of marine life forms out there.

Oceans are frequently used as a means of transport, with various companies shipping their products across oceans from one port to another.

The largest ocean on Earth is the Pacific Ocean. It covers around 30 per cent of the Earth's surface.

The Pacific Ocean's name has an original meaning of 'peaceful sea.'

The Pacific Ocean contains around 25,000 different islands; much more, than found in other oceans.

THE BERMUDA TRIANGLE

The Bermuda Triangle is located in the Atlantic Ocean.

> The location of the Bermuda Triangle is around the east coast of Florida and Peurto Rico and also a little part of it is next to South Carolina.

> The Bermuda Triangle doesn't have an actual absolute location because it is so big but is in between 80-90° west and 30-20° north.

The Bermuda Triangle has many interesting facts. Here are three of them:

The Bermuda Triangle is not actually a triangle; in fact, it doesn't even have a definite shape and it has never had an official boundary.

The Bermuda Triangle has supposedly been responsible for the disappearance of more than over sixty six planes and ships.

The Bermuda Triangle has not sucked in all the ships and planes that come near it or over it.

WEATHER FACTS

Tsunami is actually a series of waves that can travel at speeds averaging 450 (and up to 600) miles per hour in the open ocean.

> A tsunami is a series of water waves called a tsunami wave train.

The literal translation of the word 'tsunami' is harbour wave.

The origin of the word 'tsunami' comes from the Japanese language.

> The best protection following a tsunami warning is to evacuate from coastal areas or move to a third-floor level.

A tsunami is a series of waves. Do not assume that one wave means that the danger is over. The next wave may be larger than the first one. Stay out of the area.

The greatest danger is to those in areas at an elevation of less than 20 feet. Water being pushed inland by the tsunami will bring massive amounts of debris as it pushes inland, including vehicles and small buildings.

> Computer models can predict tsunami arrival, usually within minutes of the arrival time.

Natural factors such as shoreline tree cover can mitigate tsunami effects.

> Many early geological, geographical and oceanographic texts refer to tsunamis as 'seismic sea waves.'

It is true that tsunamis occasionally occur in large lakes.

Greek historian Thucydides was the first person to relate tsunamis to submarine earthquakes.

True: It is not possible to prevent a tsunami.

The Pacific Tsunami Warning System is based in Honolulu, Hawaii.

The heaviest hailstone ever recorded weighed 1 kilo gram (2.25 lb) and landed in Gopalganj District, Bangladesh on April 14, 1986.

ALLIGATORS NEVER NEED DENTURES

While both humans and alligators depend on their teeth in order to chew food, humans only get two sets of natural teeth to last them a lifetime. Alligators get from 2,000 to 3,000 teeth during the course of their lifetime!

'SALT OF THE EARTH' IS MORE THAN A TITLE

There is enough salt in the world's oceans to cover all the land on all the continents to a depth of nearly 500 feet!

IF ONLY WE COULD PLUG INTO IT!

A cloud to ground bolt of lightning carries between 100 million and 1 billion volts. It can reach 50,000 °F— three-four times hotter than the surface of the sun!

THE WORLD'S MOST DANGEROUS ANIMAL

The not-so humble mosquito wins this award hands down. Mosquitoes transmitting countless diseases kill more animals—including humans—than any other animal (or plant) on Earth.

AND DON'T DRINK THE WATER

97 per cent of the water on earth is undrinkable. An estimated 20 per cent of the world's surface fresh water supply is contained in Lake Baikal in southern Siberia (the world's deepest lake at more than a mile in depth).

NUCLEAR POWER FACTS

The word 'nuclear' is related to the nucleus of an atom; it is often used to describe the energy produced when a nucleus is split (fission) or joined with another (fusion).

The nucleus is positively charged and found at the central core of an atom.

Nuclear physics is the study of atomic nuclei and their interactions.

Nuclear power uses fission to create heat and electricity.

The US, France and Japan are the largest producers of nuclear power.

Nuclear power provides around 14 per cent of the world's electricity.

Nuclear power plants have a relatively good safety record but there is ongoing debate on the threat they pose, especially after widely publicised accidents at Chernobyl, Three Mile Island and Fukushima.

The radioactive waste produced by nuclear reactors can be difficult to dispose off safely.

The military often use nuclear reactors to power their submarines and aircraft carriers.

Nuclear weapons use the energy produced by fission or fusion to create destructive blasts.

While many nuclear weapons have been used in testing, only two have been used as part of warfare.

In August 1945, near the end of World War 2, the United States used atomic bombs on the Japanese cities of Hiroshima and Nagasaki, leading to the death of approximately 200,000 people.

Enriched uranium is a crucial element of both nuclear weapons and nuclear power production.

The Sun creates energy through the nuclear fusion of hydrogen nuclei into helium.

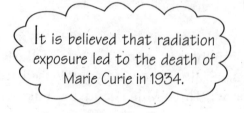

It is believed that radiation exposure led to the death of Marie Curie in 1934.

Nuclear fusion (joining atom nuclei) also has the potential for energy production.

Around 6 per cent of the world's energy and 14 per cent of the world's electricity is produced by nuclear power.

There are over 400 nuclear power reactors in use around the world.

Around thirty different countries have operational nuclear reactors.

The largest producers of nuclear power are the US, France and Japan.

Nuclear power provides around 20 per cent of the electricity used in the US.

Nuclear power plants have a relatively good safety record but there is strong debate about the potential risk they pose.

The Fukushima Daiichi nuclear disaster occurred following the Tohoku earthquake and tsunami in Japan.

The Calder Hall nuclear power station in the UK was the first to deliver commercial quantities of electricity (1956).

NUCLEAR POWER

In 1905, Einstein discovered that mass could be changed into energy and vice versa. In 1918, Sir Ernest Rutherford showed that atoms could be split. By 1942, the world had its first nuclear reactor.

Globally, there are over 430 commercial nuclear power reactors in thirty one countries

The world's first nuclear power plant to create electricity for a power grid was USSR's Obninsk Nuclear Power Plant, which opened on June 27, 1954.

A nuclear power plant must shut down every eighteen to twenty four months to remove its used uranium fuel, or radioactive waste.

The most recent nuclear test was done by North Korea on May 25, 2009.

Just removing a person's outer clothing can remove 90 per cent of the radioactive material after a disaster.

After Japan's nuclear disaster in 2011, several countries have rethought the use of nuclear energy. For example, Germany plans to close all of its reactors by 2022. Italy and Switzerland have halted expanding their nuclear power. However, some big markets, such as China and India, are still pushing ahead with new nuclear plants.

A nuclear war would kill approximately 1 billion people, and hundreds of millions would be injured. The 3-4 billion people left alive would find themselves facing widespread radioactive contamination, a possible nuclear winter, increased levels of damaging ultraviolet rays due to partial destruction of the ozone layer, a global photochemical smog, as well as a multitude of toxic pollutants.

Of the 2,000 nuclear explosions conducted worldwide between 1954 and 1996, 25 per cent (over 500 bombs) were detonated in the atmosphere. A major part of the explosions were carried out underground. In fact, 75 per cent of all nuclear tests during the Cold War were conducted underground.

Between 1955 and 1989, the average number of nuclear tests every year was fifty five.

Uranium is a source of today's nuclear fuel. During the Middle Ages, craftspeople used it to colour glass yellow or certain shades of green.

SPACE FACTS

Constantly Moving

Fact: We are moving through space at the rate of 530
   kilometre a second

GOODBYE OLD PAL!

Fact: The moon is drifting away from Earth- Every year
   the moon moves about 3.8 centimetres further away
   from the Earth. This is caused by tidal effects.

The temperature at the core of the sun is 13,600,000
   kelvins. All of the energy produced by fusion in the
   core must travel through many successive layers to
   the solar photosphere before it escapes into space as
   sunlight or kinetic energy of particles.

SOLAR DIET

Fact: The Sun loses up to a billion kilograms a second
   due to solar winds.

GEORGE'S STAR

Originally Uranus was known by this name

Astronauts are people who serve on spacecraft and fly into outer space. In Russia and the former Soviet Union, they are also known as cosmonauts. As of 2013, 530 people worldwide have gone into space.

ASTRONAUTS FACTS

The pilot or commander of a space shuttle is required to fly 1,000 hours as a jet pilot before being selected as an astronaut. He/She has to be at least 5 feet 8 inches tall to be selected for a space mission. However, astronauts can grow taller while in space, approximately up to two inches if they are there for a month. Due to lack of gravity, the spine stretches while they're in space.

It is possible for astronauts to spend a long time in space. The longest time spent living in outer space was two years and seventy three days between 1991 and 1999.

In space, it is not possible
to breathe normally, so an
astronaut's spacesuit is
outfitted with oxygen so they
can breathe when working
outside the spacecraft.

Astronauts can urinate outside the spacecraft while wearing their spacesuits. He or she will wear a maximum absorbency garment (MAG), which can hold up to 2 litres of fluid.

Astronauts sleep in bunk beds or in sleeping bags. However, these bunk beds must be fitted with buckles so the astronauts can buckle up. Otherwise, they might float around the spacecraft while sleeping.

They can choose from seventy
different types of food. However, the
food will either be prepackaged or
would need just a very small amount
of preparation. Sometimes when
astronauts are eating, the food will
float around, as there is no gravity.

Common items eaten include brownies, meat, pasta, fruit and soft drinks. Astronauts must eat fresh vegetables or fruit within two days of the launch. As they get spoilt quickly, a majority of the fruits are dried. Any meat will have to be heat-treated to kill any bacteria. Certain foods such as bread are not allowed in space as crumbs can be inhaled, get in one's eyes or damage equipment. Instead, astronauts are given Tortillas.

When not actively working, astronauts can read books, watch movies, or talk to family and friends on Earth. They can even use an exercise bike (they have to do a lot of exercise to stay healthy.)

The first living animal in orbit was a dog from Russia called Laika. She travelled into space on Sputnik 2 in 1957.

American astronauts have the dog 'Snoopy' from the comic strip *Peanuts* as their safety mascot.

There is no wind or rain in space so an astronaut's footprints on the Moon will remain for at least a million years.

SOLAR POWER FACTS

As early as 1921, the Nobel Peace Prize was awarded to Albert Einstein for experiments in solar power and photovoltaics.

When silicon is taken from just one ton of sand, and used in photovoltaic solar power panels, that silicon can produce as much electricity as 500,000 tons of burning coal.

In the U.S., there are more than 10,000 homes that get their energy entirely from solar power.

Nearly 200 years ago, a British astronomer by the name of John Herschel cooked food with solar power during a journey to Africa.

California opened its first large solar power plant in 1982.

Solar power can cut water bills by more than 50 per cent each year in a home where a solar model replaces the electric water heater.

According to the Department of Energy, the price of photovoltaic (PV) solar power panels has dropped 200 per cent over the last thirty years. Owners now pay between 10 and 40 cents per kilowatt-hour.

A study by the U.S. Department of Energy (USDOE) showed that solar power conditions were close to perfect (99 per cent) in San Francisco on June 14th, 2000. On that day, 100,000 customers in that area lost power. Solar power could have provided all they needed.

Another USDOE study showed that the roofs of California's city and county buildings, if covered with solar PV panels, could generate 200 megawatts of clean electricity! Cover California's school roofs with solar power panels, and you add 1,500 megawatts more to the state's peak power supply.

Germany is making the best use of solar power, even though its climate includes many cloudy days.

It takes only about eight minutes for solar energy to travel from the sun to the earth.

TEN ACCIDENTAL INVENTIONS

Louis Pasteur once said, 'chance favours the prepared mind.' That's the genius behind all these accidental inventions—the scientists were prepared. They did their science on the brink and were able to see the magic in a mistake, set-back, or coincidence.

1. Penicillin

Alexander Fleming didn't clean up his workstation before going on vacation one day in 1928. When he came back, Fleming noticed that there was a strange fungus on some of his cultures. Even stranger was that bacteria didn't seem to thrive near those cultures.

Penicillin became the first and is still one of the most widely used antibiotics.

2. Pacemaker

Wilson Greatbatch was working on making a circuit to help record fast heart sounds. He reached into a box for a resistor in order to finish the circuit and pulled out a 1-megaohm resistor instead of a 10,000-ohm one.

The circuit pulsed for 1.8 milliseconds and then stopped for one second. Then it repeated. The sound was as old as man: a perfect heartbeat.

3. Mauve

In 1856 Perkin was trying to come up with an artificial quinine. Instead of a malaria treatment, his experiments produced a thick murky mess. But the more he looked at it, the more Perkin saw a beautiful color in his mess. Turns out he had made the first-ever synthetic dye.

His dye was far better than any dyes that came from nature; the colour was brighter, more vibrant, and didn't fade or wash out. His discovery also turned chemistry into a money-generating science-making it attractive for a whole generation of curious-minded people.

4. Radioactivity

Becquerel realised that the uranium rock he had left in the drawer had imprinted itself on a photographic plate without being exposed to sunlight first. There was something very special about that rock. Working with Marie and Pierre Curie, he discovered that something was radioactivity.

5. Plastic

Leo Baekeland thought his 'Bakelite' might be used for phonograph records, but it was soon clear that the product had thousands of uses. Today, plastic, which was derived from Bakelite, is used for everything from telephones to iconic movie punch lines.

6. Vulcanized Rubber

Charles Goodyear one day spilled a mixture of rubber, sulfur and lead onto a hot stove. The heat charred the mixture, but didn't ruin it. When Goodyear picked up the accident, he noticed that the mixture had hardened but was still quite usable.

At last! The breakthrough he had been waiting for! His vulcanized rubber is used in everything from tires, to shoes, to hockey pucks.

7. Teflon

Young DuPont chemist Roy Plunkett was working to make a new a new kind of CFC. He had a theory that if he could get a compound called TFE to react with hydrochloric acid, he could produce the refrigerant he wanted.

Only it hadn't. Frustrated and angry, Plunkett took off the top of the canister and shook it. Out came some fine white flakes. Luckily for everyone who's ever made an omelet, he was intrigued by the flakes and handed them off to other scientists at DuPont.

8. Coke

Atlanta pharmacist John Pemberton was trying to make a cure for headaches. He mixed together a bunch of ingredients -- and don't ask, because we don't know; The recipe is still a closely guarded secret. It only took eight years of being sold in a drug store before the drink was popular enough to be sold in bottles.

9. Smart Dust

Jamie Link was doing her doctoral work in chemistry at the University of California, San Diego when one of the silicon chips she was working on burst. She discovered afterward, however, that the tiny pieces still functioned as sensors.

The resulting 'smart dust' can be used to monitor the purity of drinking or seawater, to detect hazardous chemical or biological agents in the air, or to locate and destroy tumour cells in the body.

10. Saccharin

> Saccharin, the sweetener in the pink packet, was discovered because chemist Constantin Fahlberg didn't wash his hands after a day at the office.

The year was 1879 and Fahlberg was trying to come up with new and interesting uses for coal tar. After a productive day at the office, he went home and something strange happened.

> He noticed the rolls he was eating tasted particularly sweet. The next day he went back to the lab and started tasting his work until he found the sweet spot.

MORE POTPOURRI

> The risk of being struck by a falling meteorite for a human is one occurrence every 9,300 years

A thimbleful of a neutron star would weigh over 100 million tons.

Blood sucking hookworms inhabit 700 million people worldwide.

We can produce laser light a million times brighter than sunshine.

The combined length of the roots of a Finnish pine tree is over 30 miles.

60-65 million years ago dolphins and humans shared a common ancestor.

The evaporation from a large oak or beech tree is from 10 to 25 gallons in twenty four hours.

AMAZING DISCOVERIES

Quantum Computer on A Single CPU

Matteo Mariantoni and colleagues were the first to implement a quantum version of the 'Von Neumann' architecture found in home computers. Its creation helps to move us closer to the development of practical quantum computers that can solve real-life problems and help move us into the 21st century.

Neandrathal Genes Survive in Us

The study determined that some of the human X chromosome originated from Neanderthals, but only in people of non-African heritage.

Potentially Habitable, Earth-Like Planet Found

With a radius 2.4 times that of Earth, NASA scientists have confirmed that Kepler-22b is the first planet ever discovered that orbits its sun within the so-called 'Goldilocks Zone.' This makes it the most Earth-like planet to be discovered.

Measuring The Universe With Black Holes

Darach Watson and colleagues have worked out a way to use supermassive black holes—which exist at the center of most galaxies—as 'standard candles' for making accurate measurements of cosmic distances.

Flushing Senescent Cells

Gerontologists showed in November, that flushing aged, broken-down cells from the bodies of mice indeed slowed down their aging. This was powerful proof that so-called 'cellular senescence' did matter.

Photosynthetic Protein Captured

Researchers in Japan have mapped, in striking detail, the structure of the Photosystem II protein, a protein that plants use to split water into oxygen and hydrogen.

World's First Malaria Vaccine

Scientists at the Oxford University developed the world's first vaccine against the malaria parasite which has been shown to be effective against even the most deadliest strains.

Hints of the Higgs Boson

The LHC may have found what it was looking for in December 2012 when results from two experiments showed a small data bump in their results which just might be the elusive 'God Particle' – the Higgs Boson.

Faster Than Light Particles

Researchers at OPERA announced in September that they had measured neutrinos travelling faster than light.

HIV Treatment For Prevention

The journal *Science* has named the HIV study, known as HPTN 052, as the most important scientific breakthrough of 2011. The clinical trial of the treatment showed that people with HIV are 96 per cent less likely to transmit the virus to their partners if they take antiretroviral drugs (ARVs).

COMPUTER FUN FACTS

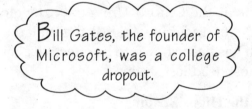

Bill Gates, the founder of Microsoft, was a college dropout.

On eBay, one of the world's most popular shopping websites, there are transactions of approximately $680 per second.

There are approximately 6,000 new computer viruses released every month.

The E-mail is older than the World Wide Web.

Doug Engelbart, invented the first computer mouse in 1964. It was made of wood!

One of the world's leading computer and computer peripheral manufacturers, Hewlett Packard, first started in a garage at Palo Alto in 1939.

If you open up the case of the original Macintosh, you will find forty seven signatures, which is of each member of Apple's Macintosh division of 1982.

Amongst the most interesting computer facts is, that the first Apple computer which was built by Steve Jobs and Steve Wozniak, using parts they got for free from their employers. They were made to scrounge for spare parts at work.

If you want to get a computer aquarium, then you must get the Macquariums which are aquariums made from old Macintosh computers.

It is believed that the first computer virus released in the world was a boot sector virus, which was created in 1986 by Farooq Alvi brothers. It was designed by them to protect their research work.

The group of twelve engineers who designed IBM PC were called 'The Dirty Dozen.'

A normal human being blinks twenty times in a minute, whereas a computer user blinks only seven times a minute!

The house of Bill Gates was designed using a Macintosh computer.

At 75 per cent, Sweden has the highest percentage of Internet users.

Mosaic was the first popular web browser released in the year 1993.

Since the time the game Tetrisit was created in the early eighties, it has sold more than 40 million copies worldwide, which made its creator richer by $8 million.

Almost all computer users must know how destructive a virus can be. But then, it would be interesting to know that a virus cannot corrupt your PC on its own. It corrupts your system only when you activate it by either downloading infected files from the Internet or by sharing these infected files.

Computer circuitry can be destroyed by static electricity. It is so mild for humans that they don't even feel it.

The Nvidia GeForce 6800 Ultra chip has the maximum number of transistors on it; approximately 222 million.

KonradZuse has the credit of creating the world's first computer known as the Z1 in 1936. Three years later the first fully functioning electro-mechanical computer known as Z2 was developed.

Stewardesses is the longest word which can be typed with only the left hand.

MORE FUN...

Carl Linnaeus is credited with inventing the classification system of all the animals and plants on the planet.

J. Robert Oppenheimer was the scientist in charge of the Manhattan Project during World War II.

Charles Darwin traced the discrepancy between the developments of different species of finches in the Galapagos Islands.

By the year 2012, there will be approximately 17 billion devices connected to the Internet.

Philosopher Ptolemy was credited with discovering the geocentric theory of the universe.

My Space reports over 110 million registered users. Were it a country, it would be the tenth largest, just behind Mexico.

> One of every eight married couples in the US last year met online.

The average twenty one year old has spent 5,000 hours playing video games, has exchanged 250,000 e-mails, instant and text messages and has spent 10,000 hours on the mobile phone.

Dresden Codex shows early records of solar eclipse tables, comet movement and planets documented by members of the Mayan civilization.

The first banner advertising was used in 1994.

> The first domain name ever registered was Symbolics.com.

There are approximately 1,319,872,109 people on the Internet.

> There are approximately 1.06 billion instant messaging accounts worldwide.

While it took the radio thirty eight years, and the television a short thirteen years, it took the World Wide Web only four years to reach 50 million users.

70 per cent of virus writers work under contract for organized crime syndicates.

A program named 'Rother J' was the first computer virus to come into sight 'in the wild'—that is, outside the single computer or lab where it was created.

The worst MS-DOS virus ever, Michelangelo (1991), attacks the boot sector of your hard drive and any floppy drive inserted into the computer, which causes the virus to spread rapidly.

THE SCIENCE OF THE BODY

APPENDIX TO LIFE

It is usually treated as a body part that lost its function millions of years ago. All it seems to do is occasionally get infected and cause appendicitis. Yet recently it has been discovered that the appendix is very useful to the bacteria that help your digestive system function.

SUPERSIZED MOLECULES

The biggest molecule in nature resides in your body. It is chromosome 1. A normal human cell has twenty three pairs of chromosomes in its nucleus, each a single, very long, molecule of DNA. Chromosome 1 is the biggest, containing around ten billion atoms, to pack in the amount of information that is encoded in the molecule.

ATOM COUNT

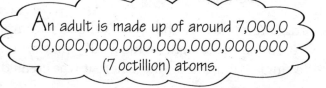

An adult is made up of around 7,000,0 00,000,000,000,000,000,000,000 (7 octillion) atoms.

FUR LOSS

It might seem hard to believe, but we have about the same number of hairs on our bodies as a chimpanzee. It's just that our hairs are useless, so fine they are almost invisible.

GOOSEBUMP EVOLUTION

Goosepimples are a remnant of our evolutionary predecessors. They occur when tiny muscles around the base of each hair tense, pulling the hair more erect. With a decent covering of fur, this would fluff up the coat, getting more air into it, making it a better insulator. But with a human's thin body hair, it just makes our skin look strange.

SPACE TRAUMA

Although liquids do boil in a vacuum, your blood is kept under pressure by your circulatory system and would be just fine. And although space is very cold, you would not lose heat particularly quickly. As thermos flasks demonstrate, vacuum is a great insulator. In practice, the thing that will kill you in space is simply the lack of air.

ATOMIC COLLAPSE

The nucleus that makes up the vast bulk of matter in an atom is much smaller than the whole structure that it is comparable to the size of a fly in a cathedral. If you lost all your empty atomic space, your body would fit into a cube less than 1/500th of a centimetre on each side.

ELECTROMAGNETIC REPULSION

This electromagnetic force is vastly stronger than the force of gravity—around a billion, billion, billion, billion times stronger. You can demonstrate the relative strength by holding a fridge magnet near a fridge and letting go. The electromagnetic force from the tiny magnet overwhelms the gravitational attraction of the whole Earth.

STARDUST TO STARDUST

Every atom in your body is billions of years old. Hydrogen, the most common element in the universe and a major feature of your body, was produced in the Big Bang 13.7 billion years ago. Heavier atoms such as carbon and oxygen were forged in stars between 7 billion and 12 billion years ago, and blasted across space when the stars exploded. Some of these explosions were so powerful that they also produced the elements heavier than iron, which stars can't construct. This means that the components of your body are truly ancient: you are stardust.

THE QUANTUM BODY

One of the mysteries of science is how something as apparently solid and straightforward as your body can be made of strangely behaving quantum particles such as atoms and their constituents. In reality, electrons are confined to specific orbits, as if they ran on rails. They can't exist anywhere between these orbits but have to make a 'quantum leap' from one to another.

RED BLOODED

The red colour arises because the iron is bound in a ring of atoms in haemoglobin called porphyrin and it's the shape of this structure that produces the colour.

Just how red your haemoglobin is depends on whether there is oxygen bound to it. The presence of oxygen changes the shape of the porphyrin, giving the red blood cells a more vivid shade.

GOING VIRAL

Surprisingly, not all the useful DNA in your chromosomes comes from your evolutionary ancestors – some of it was borrowed from elsewhere. Your DNA includes the genes from at least eight retroviruses.

OTHER LIFE

On sheer count of cells, there is more bacterial life inside you than human. There are around 10 trillion of your own cells, but ten times more bacteria. Many of the bacteria that call you home are friendly in the sense that they don't do any harm. Some are beneficial.

EYELASH INVADERS

Depending on how old you are, it's pretty likely that you have eyelash mites. These tiny creatures live on old skin cells and the natural oil (sebum) produced by human hair follicles. They are usually harmless, though they can cause an allergic reaction in a minority of people.

PHOTON DETECTORS

Your eyes are very sensitive, able to detect just a few photons of light. If you take a look on a very clear night at the constellation of Andromeda, a little fuzzy patch of light is just visible with the naked eye. If you can make out that tiny blob, you are seeing as far as is humanly possible without technology.

SENSORY TALLY

Despite what you've probably been told, you have more than five senses. Here's a simple example. Put your hand a few centimetres away from a hot iron. None of your five senses can tell you the iron will burn you. Yet you can feel that the iron is hot from a distance and won't touch it. This is thanks to an extra sense – the heat sensors in your skin. Similarly, we can detect pain or tell if we are upside down.

Genes are only a tiny part of our DNA. The other 97 per cent was thought to be junk until recently, but we now realise that epigenetics – the processes that go on outside the genes – also have a major influence on our development.

REAL AGE

Just like a chicken, your life started off with an egg. However, there is a significant difference between a human egg and a chicken egg that has a surprising effect on your age.

> Human eggs are tiny. They are, after all, just a single cell and are typically around 0.2 millimetres across – about the size of a printed full stop.

CONSCIOUS ACTION

> If you are like most people, you will locate your conscious mind roughly behind your eyes, as if there was a little person sitting there, steering the much larger automaton that is your body. In reality, much of the control comes from your unconscious.

OPTICAL DELUSION

The picture of the world we 'see' is artificial. Our brains don't produce an image the way a video camera works. Instead, the brain constructs a model of the world from the information provided by modules that measure light and shade, edges, curvature and so on. This makes it simple for the brain to paint out the blind spot, the area of your retina where the optic nerve joins, which has no sensors.

EINSTEIN FUN!

As he didn't talk until he was four, his parents were worried about him. But once while they were on the supper table, he broke his four-year silence and said 'The soup is too hot.'

He never loved haircuts and wearing socks while sailing and violin were his passions. He named his violin Lina.

After Einstein's death, his brain was removed from his head without his family's knowledge. This immoral act was done by Dr. Thomas Harvey who wanted to conduct a search on his brain. He was later permitted by Einstein's son Hans Einstein.

He had a very bad memory and he could not remember dates and phone numbers, in fact he even didn't knew what his own phone number was.

Once his mathematics professor called him a lazy dog because he could not find Einstein's interest in studies.

He was inspired by a compass which was gifted to him by his father while he was sick at age of five. It was the start of his interest in science.

In 1952, he was offered the presidency of Israel but he politely refused the offer.

Almost all of his work is remarkable, but he got unimaginable fame when his paper on mass-energy equivalence was published.

He used to charge people for his autograph and donate all this money to charity.

In 1951, while leaving a party with his friends, he was approached by a photographer who asked him to smile for a photograph. But Einstein who was already tired, just stuck his tongue out instead of a smile. The photographer luckily captured this memorable moment.

MEET THE ROBOTS

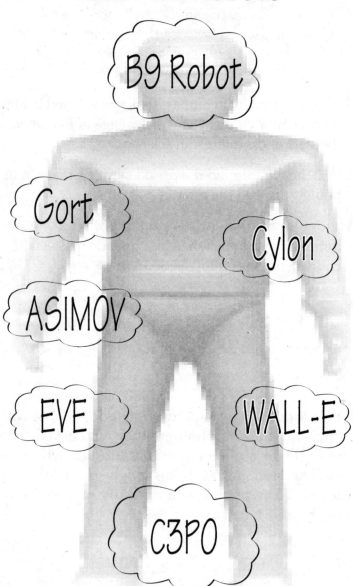